POEMS

POEMS

BY

ROBERT CONQUEST

LONDON
MACMILLAN & CO LTD
NEW YORK · ST MARTIN'S PRESS
1955

MACMILLAN AND COMPANY LIMITED
London Bombay Calcutta Madras Melbourne

THE MACMILLAN COMPANY OF CANADA LIMITED
Toronto

ST MARTIN'S PRESS INC
New York

PRINTED IN GREAT BRITAIN

In Memory of

MAURICE LANGLOIS

poet,

died in the hands of the

secret police of the occupying power.

Most of these poems have appeared in the following periodicals or anthologies, to which acknowledgement is due : *The Listener, The New Statesman and Nation, Tribune, World Review, The Spectator, Encounter, London Magazine, Poems 1951* and *New Poems 1952, 1953* and *1954.*

CONTENTS

I

PERSONS AND PLACES

II

ARTS AND CONTEXTS

III

WAR AND AFTER

IV

THE BALKANS

I

PERSONS AND PLACES

Nantucket

It lay in the mist or the wind.

Perhaps Karlsefni saw it to starboard
On the voyage to Hóp from Straumfjord.

Fishermen, farmers and theologians
Settled the swept bay and the crescent bluffs.

And then its attention was filled with whales.
A blunt, chipped sickle : it reaped the sea.
Oh, that was an astonishing empire !
All the oceans gave up to its hunters
Dangerous and profitable monsters.
Folgers and Husseys, Starbucks and Coffins,
Branded the salt wrath with their keels and spears.

Melville chose them, the boldest men on earth,
To be his champions on the demon seas
Of his heart.   Even they succumbed.
Ahab died.   The waters washed
The ruined survivor to another coast.

The whaling went elsewhere, to techniques and guns.
And the island lies in its parish, weather and past.

Guided Missiles Experimental Range

SOFT sounds and odours brim up through the night
A wealth below the level of the eye ;
Out of a black, an almost violet sky
Abundance flowers into points of light.

Till from the south-west, as their low scream mars
And halts this warm hypnosis of the dark,
Three black automata cut swift and stark,
Shaped clearly by the backward flow of stars.

Stronger than lives, by empty purpose blinded,
The only thought their circuits can endure is
The target-hunting rigour of their flight ;

And by that loveless haste I am reminded
Of Aeschylus' description of the Furies :
' *O barren daughters of the fruitful night.*'

Stendhal's Consulate

He already knows everything that needs to be known.
He has examined his life : his gifts have been shown.
    Immensely capable, he looks from his niche
      Wishing he were reasonably rich.

Reverencing art and love only, still his critique
Does not exempt their instruments or their technique.
    And even in this hot, boring town
      He can still write life down,

Demonstrating what, he feels, must already be plain
To the intelligent and even the sensitive : that life can
      contain
    A hardness society's verminous power
      May savage but cannot devour.

With evasion and skill he is not wholly separate from
Giulia Rinieri, the music of Mozart, or Rome.
    And with an occasional testing glance
      He continues to watch for his chance.

And his calm gaze penetrates poets' and nations' rage
Expecting us too to be, even in this hot age,
    Fairly resigned to our portions of
      That alloy of failure and love.

Background Music

SUMMER in Copenhagen ; light on green spires.
Once a philosopher walked beneath these lindens
Thinking : 'Man through imagination enters
The real ; ideas and women are its lures.'

— The life-bound in the sexual act set free
Or in a woman's ambience, split their instants
To quanta from the edge of Time's existence,
And enter the concept of eternity.

Not only that : it gives the landscape form,
And is the immanence of every art.
    — Yet though in this green day the idea is yours

It stammers in me to expound in verse
A philosophy deriving from the calm
As you move into the centre of my heart.

Catullus at Sirmio (56 B.C.)

AT Sirmio, peninsula and island,
It's winter now. The willows are like iron ;
A little snow lies in the furrows ; and mist hides
The far part of the lake's grey shield :
— Not my sort of weather. Light
Comes through the low and heavy sky
With the unequal glare and blur of ice.
Some poet could get beauty out of it, perhaps :
The vaguely outlined mountains, even this blasted wind
Whipping the water.
                              Bring me some hot wine.
This sort of weather's like Caesar,
Single-mindedness with a few cold contrary gusts
— Perversions. I've written about that. He says
I've given him ill-fame for ever. But
He'll get power (if that wet Pompey doesn't)
And then he'll get poets. Still, it's satisfactory
That he minds my cuts : *I* wouldn't. It's the relics
Of shame before the civilized. It'll pass.

Beauty indeed — give me the guts of it — passion ;
And pride if you will. Sweetness I've sought,
The lyrics of simple guiltless lust.
But it was always nonsense. I found the poem
And hid the truth in it ; which was fair enough.
Look at Clodia : breath-taking breasts ;
A green sweat of pleasure ; and my heart whipped
By her bitchiness like this lake by wind — there's beauty !
— But there are worse things : to be frozen
Into the deep black ice of Caesar's epoch.
Oh, they'll fix it. The people want peace and quiet.

7

They'll back the thug up to dictator ;
If they must have such leaders, let them rot.
Poets will write about victories and buildings,
Tack bits of beauty on to the rulers' conscience
Or do exercises to order about their hearts.

It's a bit warmer.
Noon loosens the water ; the stream flows more freely ;
The trees unstiffen ; the leaves' tongues move and speak.
Beauty, I was saying. Well, what have I got ?
I'll die young and with nothing to show for it
But a few verses and a few brilliant nights
And endless irritation.
— Yet one can't calculate. Timidity and trade
Aren't for Valerians. And I couldn't live in
The ages of disgust ahead. The great make me sick.
Women are whores. And poems ? — it's not as a poet
      I'm proud.
Still, there may be others of me later. Damn posterity ;
Let *them* read my stuff, if Caesar's boys don't burn it.
In their minds let my pride revel ; and my revenge.

A Girl in the Snow

FOR T.

AUTUMN'S attrition. Then this world laid waste
Under a low white sky, diffusing glare
On blurs of snow as motionless and bare
As the dead epoch where our luck is placed.

Till from the imprecise close distance flies,
Winged on your skis and stillness-breaking nerve
Colour, towards me down this vital curve,
Blue suit, bronze hair and honey-coloured eyes.

Under this hollow cloud, a sky of rime,
The eyes' one focus in an empty mirror
You come towards my arms until I hold

Close to my heart, beyond all fear and error,
A clear-cut warmth in this vague waste of cold :
A road of meaning through the shapeless time.

Lake Success

FALL in Long Island :
Deep in the dying fires of beech and sumach
Under a motionless air holding vapour
Invisible but enough to filter the sun
From a rage of light to a source of clarity,
In these buildings there is talk of peace.

In the Security Council and the six Committees,
In the air-conditioned ambience and too-ideal lighting,
A notoriously maladministered state is smug about man-
    dates,
The sponsor of an aggressor utters pacific phrases,
A state ruled by a foreign marshal condemns colonial
    oppression,
A middle-easterner makes a statesmanlike speech in very
    elegant French.

These little men, vain and silly, tough and intelligent,
    cunning and mean,
Good and patient, selfish and loud, cultured and weak,
Are here distinguished by a different standard of value :
One represents twenty-five thousand tanks,
One speaks with the voice of a whole potential continent,
One has successfully resisted the will of a powerful neigh-
    bour,
One of the most impressive is merely an empty voice.

Miles away to the west, high in the air which is
A pale single fluid, the summits of great buildings
Glitter like masked and very distant snow ;
In the foreground, outside the vacant lawns,

Amazingly vivid leaves are slowly falling ;
And in here, in a sense at the heart of the human world,
These tangibles are merely memory,
And paper and words are immediately real.   And yet,
In this web of power and propaganda, sufficient
Devotion and intelligence are assembled
To ensure at least a painstaking effort to see
That the chances of peace may not (and that bombs may
    not)
Fall in Long Island.

To a Girl who Dreamt about a Poem

SOFTLY, beneath a scarcely trembling starlight,
A blue sleep rises and engulfs her bed.
That sweet intelligence, transfigured only,
Distils its music in the pillowed head.

The soft night air, through pastures of a legend,
Lets her unmoving body drift along
A tide of flutes.   That clear imagination
Sways like a dancer to the unheard song.

But formal resonances of those lines
Arguing aspects of a view of art
Take up the ground-bass, their crude rhythms softened
To beat in concord with that sleeping heart.

And I ask her to believe no sort of praises
Could raise them further in the poet's esteem
Than if I honestly could think those verses
Deserved admittance to the gracious dream.

The Landing in Deucalion[1]

SCREENED by the next few decades from our vision
Their image, none the less, is fairly clear,
Emerging from the air-lock into light
Sharp, unfamiliar in its composition,
From cold stars and a small blue flaming sun
As glints of racing Phobos disappear.

Leaving the rocket pointing at that sky
Their steps and sight turn to the chosen spot
Through this thin air through which the thin winds keen ;
The valves hiss in their helmets as they cross
The crumbling sand towards the belt of green
Where long-sought strangeness will reveal — what ?

And why this subject should be set to verse
Is only partly in what fuels their hearts
More powerful than those great atomic drives
(Resembling as it does the thrust of poetry —
The full momentum of the poets' whole lives)
— Its consummation is yet more like art's :

For as they reach that unknown vegetation
Their thirst is given satisfaction greater
Than ever found but when great arts result ;
Not just new detail or a changed equation
But freshly flaming into all the senses
And from the full field of the whole gestalt.

And so I sing them now, as others later.

[1] *Deucalionis Regio*, the area to the south of the Sinus Sabaeus, on Mars.

13

Adriatic

(i)

As the poem drifts under the cry of the sea
He drowns beneath its images of water,
   The brilliant foam unfrozen
   Out of a fatal pearl.

At once, uncontrolledly blown by the black wind
The images try to make their own poem
   And the whole Id flowers
   In a tumultuous rose.

He must seek other waters, the chalk stream,
The Maggiore blue, or even in desert moments
   The tang of a brackish fountain,
   But still the water of life.

(ii)

Requiring no agony of accuracy
Its method of completeness sets against
   The white wake of a ship
   The whole harmonious sea.

(iii)

Into its essence, then, the poem must welcome
The natural luminosities and idylls :
   A sea as cool as glass,
   Monte Gargano's blue ridge ;

The greatness of soul of all great writers must
Haunt and inform it, their close approach to freedom,
    Like Turgenev creating
    The world from a girl's tears ;

Yes, all sensuousness and scepticism
Formed under discipline and passion into
    The Apollonian and Dionysian
    Intensities of light and darkness . . .

The sun instils solidity and shallowness
Into these formed rocks and this living sea
    And below it lies a land
    Of the usual trees and passions,

And these rich materials await their shaper
To create among its scaldings and obsessions
    The clear Promethean spirit
    Through a broken, tragic age.

A Woman Poet

THE superficial graces go,
And yet such grace remains
About that bare iambic flow
Although the syntax strains
To a tense symmetry, and so
Remotely entertains
    The thundering percussion

Out of the distant heartbeat caught
And never turned away,
Though hidden in a careful thought
No image would delay,
If any image could support
A femininity
    Made flame to purge its vision :

Which saw that fair correcting hand
Resolve the faults of love
In a sweet calculus that spanned
The diapason of
All that a mind could understand
Or mindless music move
    Of passion and compassion.

Near Jakobselv

DWARF willow, bilberry, bogcotton ; a land of lakes,
And to the north a flat transparent ocean
That stretches to the ice-cap. For those millions
Of frozen tons are always somewhere there,
Though out of sight now and far at the back of the mind
In the long hot day and the green efflorescence.

The insects pipe and drone. The arctic sky,
A very pale blue, completely bare of cloud,
Lays down its haunting midnight on the tundra.
There is no human trace for hours behind us,
And now we lie and sleep, or watch the new

Arctic world that rises like a mayfly
Out of each melting winter and never grows old,
But dies. Nothing here
Is in connexion with the central planet,
With the long histories and the human vision.

Its images are not ours. This speed and brightness
Are innocent of purpose. And in that huge returning
Winter that waits in the north there is no moral
— The ice bears no relation to the anger.
I lie and listen

To the desolating cry of an eagle.
                              Perhaps
This very newness and this isolation
May strike some hidden tremor in the heart
And make its rock gush water.

My companion
Sleeps, scarcely breathing, on the blue-green lichen.
And a faint unchanging radiance plays on us
Out of the whole young landscape, as I lie and watch for
hours
The motionless lake and the grebe diving.

The Death of Hart Crane

At first his own effortless high tension
Could match and move the edged electric city,
While under the great bridge sloped the waves,
Flat, tamed, shimmering with oil,
Vestigial to the dying endless sea.

O Queen's, keep off the killing wind.
O Bronx, bring close the seasons and the soil.
O Brooklyn and Richmond, let the sea come through.
And O Manhattan, Manhattan, root and live.

For years the raving city fattened on
Protein of his, as of a million hearts,
But the silent hunger of the sea went on.

Yet if Manhattan by an effort of will
Slowed down for thirty seconds for a prayer
It would no longer be the mindless city
Which, irritating, hurting, driving him to die,
Was none the less his only home.

Blinded at last by neon dawn
He sought the sea with different images,
All the lost galleons and the gazing seals.

But between the Bacardi ports he found that though
The city had too much and meaningless action
The sea had too much death.

Anthéor

A HEAVY light hangs in these silent airs.
Out to the west the failing day prepares
A sultry splendour.   Lying on the cliff
I watch the little bay below, the beach,
Red rocks, the slow vibrations of the sea,
Gazing deep into it all as if
   I could find beneath it the truth
   And be free.

What can a poem do with a landscape ?   What
Extract that pure philosophies cannot ?
Express the universe in terms of parts
Chosen to illustrate all time and space,
Deducing then beyond those images
The general essence of all human hearts
   And the most transitory look
   On a face ?

The emblems are too crude.   The poetry sees
A giant static set-piece where the trees'
Variety shows a single streak of green,
Or overcharged intense cosmographies
Where the light becomes too fluid, spills and soaks,
Washing away the landscape's flickering screen,
   And the hot stars crackle
   In a sky of ice.

Even the parts escape the dying words.
How can they seize precisely on that bird's
White spiral past the bastion of red rock ?
Even the redness is too subtle for

The inexact impressions of a phrase
That draws strength only from the hard-won stock
   Of image flowering from
   Our speech's core.

But word and image, the whole outer song
Can only live as surface to the strong
Thrust of the poet's whole self and language into
Perfection of his knowledge and his life,
Which unintentioned still selects the detail
From sense and vision which may help it win to
   Its own interpretation of
   That hieroglyph.

And yet each day provides its contribution
Of vision to constructing that solution.
And working, upon these red cliffs today,
To let the static and the moving reach
Their place inside one complex of relations,
I find a tentative image in the bay :
   It is the waves of the sea
   On its beach.

II
ARTS AND CONTEXTS

Poem for Julian Symons

A NOT uncommon image nags the verse
(Burke made it grace from dead religions' clash)
— Lacrima Christi from Vesuvius :
Wine out of ash.

Till the excitement of a myth proclaims
Their opposition as the emblem of
Something like the calm of Keats's poems
And the rage of his love.

But I remember, as the image gropes,
That any thirst might relish even more
A vintage pressed out of such gentle slopes
As the Côte d'Or.

For, like all images, this ash-born wine
Is no reliable or fruitful start
For anyone attempting to define
The problems of art.

The Rokeby Venus

LIFE pours out images, the accidental
At once deleted when the purging mind
Detects their resonance as inessential :
Yet these may leave some fruitful trace behind.

Thus on this painted mirror is projected
The shield that rendered safe the Gorgon's head.
A travesty. — Yet even as reflected
The young face seems to strike us, if not dead,

At least into an instantaneous winter
Which life and reason can do nothing with,
Freezing the watcher and the painting into
A single immobility of myth.

But underneath the pigments' changeless weather
The artist only wanted to devise
A posture that could show him, all together,
Face, shoulders, waist, delectable smooth thighs.

So with the faulty image as a start
We come at length to analyse and name
The luminous darkness in the depths of art :
The timelessness that holds us is the same

As that of the transcendent sexual glance
And art grows brilliant in the light it sheds,
Direct or not, on the inhabitants
Of our imaginations and our beds.

Significant Form

UNDERNEATH a rose hemisphere
Or by a river of instrumental stars
We search inside the dawn's and dark's strangeness,
And to our bodies' touch comes clear
That under its tangible bars
Still simmer all the essences and dangers.

Until in a grave resolution
It speaks the whole air's fluency and sex,
A snow of gold down from the rainless cirrus :
And we see in clear and passionate fusion
The purity of image love selects
Out of the glass-green sea and the sky's mirrors.

A Painting by Paul Klee

O LIKE the shadows now in Plato's cave
The flower throws its outline on the canvas screen
In a grey landscape where each stone
Is as receptive as an eye,
The meticulous petals lying flat and still.

And the sky is calm ; the moon resembles
A glass cave hollowed from the neutral night,
And holds through an agony of silence,
Hearing invisible dust falling,
This bitter fragile lightning and pool of stars.

I see him outline love like an abstract
As with a surgeon's delicacy now
He lays upon the canvas membrane
With a very narrow brush

The coldest colour of the heart.

Dédée d'Anvers

AROUND the iron bed the camera moves
Or follows where, across the fog-wet stone
She and her life, like one automaton,
Run to exhaustion down the usual grooves.

Quick with desire to glimpse the unobsessed,
It switches restlessly from view to view,
Pauses an instant on a seeming clue ;
Rejects it ; and resumes its nervous quest.

Till in that trajectory of fear and boredom,
Letting the iron twilight slip and slough,
Life burns through briefly to its inch of freedom

And in the flicker of a lens or eye
Forms to one microcosm of all love
A woman's body and her fantasy.

A Level of Abstraction

SUMMER, stream and stillness :
A solstice of the heart
Where she calls to its fullness
That endless search, that art.

The clear sweet known stream
Could not abstract to absolute
Crystal : he broke from that dream
A heart made desolate
In preparation for
Extremes of fruitfulness.

Briefly a kingfisher
Slashes the motionless
Vision of soft grey water
Where grey-green willows bend,
With violent speed and colour.

And yet is congruent
To blue deep clarities
Of a delighting mind
As he looks deep into eyes
Through which strong virtues bind
Into the body's grace
The reciprocal beauties
Of her heart and face.

The apparatus of paradise
Is here, is made their own.
Roses and dragonflies
Glow on water or lawn ;

The gold leaf does not move ;
The soft air has not stirred ;
She stands, the form of love.

Love is a general word.

The Classical Poets

HERBERT and Vaughan had been able to note in the study
Occasional brilliance that shook through the depths of a
    soul,
And, later, romantics readily slashed into poetry
The mountain-top flares from hearts made of tinder or coal.

It was different for these : they could energize only by
    angers
Their clear illustrations of aspects of truth which were well
Understood. Tears would burn through the crystal : to
    sing about Orpheus
Nor question his motives, who had descended to Hell.

They accepted. They valued the lake at its glittering
    surface ;
Yet their hearts were too deep. Though they ordered all
    doubt to disperse
They were poets, and they could not be wholly exempt
    from its urges
To open the weirs on their taut or magnificent verse.

With descriptions of reason or nymphs or military glory
They corrected the impulse. And, for the whole of their
    lives,
Like the mermaid on land in the Hans Andersen story,
Pretending to notice nothing, they walked upon knives.

Reading Poetry after a Quarrel

Now the brain's tightnesses unclench
   Into the timeless forms
Where the golden leaf and the snow-bud
Hang from the always-springtime branch.

And that translucence of the best
   Even among its storms
Rebuilds the great impervious dream
On which the world's foundations rest.

The Psychokinetic Experiments of Professor Rhine

THE hysteric hears the pin crash to the floor
Two rooms away ; refines his nerves so much
They can be tortured by a feather's touch ;
Or from his thought-split flesh the blood may pour ;

Or Shackleton can name the thought-of card
Before that thought has got into a mind :
They cry for systems to be redesigned
Where thought and time break down a logic's guard.

And now, the will diverts the falling dice :
Fresh discords from those future harmonies
Break the experimental frontiers' calm.

And arts may learn that we are back with Kant
Who said he would as little understand
Halting the Moon as moving his own arm.

Epistemology of Poetry

ACROSS the long-curved bight or bay
The waves move clear beneath the day
And, rolling in obliquely, each
Unwinds its white torque up the beach.

Beneath the full semantic sun
The twisting currents race and run.
Words and evaluations start.
And yet the verse should play its part.

Below a certain threshold light
Is insufficient to excite
Those mechanisms which the eye
Constructs its daytime objects by :

A different system wakes behind
The dark, wide pupils till the mind
Accepts an image of this sea
As clear, but in an altered key.

Now darkness falls.   And poems attempt
Light reconciling done and dreamt.
I do not find it in the rash
Disruption of the lightning flash.

Those vivid rigours stun the verse
And neural structure still prefers
The moon beneath whose moderate light
The great seas glitter in the bight.

Mating Season

Now love and summer hold.
Birds sleep.   A distant bell
Informs the fading air
Out of this evening gold.
Yet still the midday's glare
Aches in the failing well.

And now a sunset wind
Shakes sweetness from the trees
And off the stream's surface ;
But blows back in the mind
How the best season suffers
The air's worst agonies.

In March our birds unwinter
Against creative sleets,
But have less strength when this
Close outspoken thunder
Utters its energies
Into the withering heats.

— An image comes that shocks,
So hostile to our love
The purpose it fulfils :
Across the parching rocks
A scorpion stalks and kills
The soft exhausted dove.

Humanities

HYPNOTIZED and told they're seeing red
When really looking at a yellow wall
The children speak of orange seen instead :
Split to such rainbow through that verbal lens
It takes a whole heart's effort to see all
The human plenum as a single ens.

The word on the objective breath must be
A wind to winnow the emotive out ;
Music can generalize the inner sea
In dark harmonics of the blinded heart ;
But, hot with certainty and keen with doubt,
Verse sweats out heartfelt knowledge, clear-eyed art.

Is it, when paper roses make us sneeze,
A mental or a physical event ?
The word can freeze us to such categories,
Yet verse can warm the mirrors of the word
And through their loose distortions represent
The scene, the heart, the life, as they occurred.

— In a dream's blueness or a sunset's bronze
Poets seek the images of love and wonder,
But absolutes of music, gold or swans
Are only froth unless they go to swell
That harmony of science pealing under
The poem's waters like a sunken bell.

Another Klee

SLICED to a section for the microscope
And stained to fit the habits of the eye,
Which must deduce this sun upon its sky
Circumference to disc and disc to globe,

The shock of art has stopped the moving parts :
The shadow-fish, caught in its needled fins,
Drifts through a sea of unperspectived lines
That cannot be distinguished from its charts.

That cool expanse of unapparent water
Dissolves the stains left by creative violence
And lies untensed along the canvas wove,

But six short lines are locked upon its silence
Seeming an unknown written character
To express what this strange culture means by
        'love'.

' Head of a Faun ' by Salvator Rosa

WITH brilliant eyes and quick brown face out-thrust
Against the varnish glaze that holds him far
He leans one moment from the world of legend,
A reassuring and unhurried glimpse
    Pausing between two nymphs
    And unselfconscious lust.
Friendly, uncondescending, self-sufficient
But never breaking into the depths of the heart
He comes to intelligence and gives his message :
' We met once in a brothel or a bar '.
Well, we meet again in what is, after all, art.

A Problem

LIGURIA tingles with peculiar light.
The sea and sky exchange their various blues.
The asphodel that even goats refuse
   Glows dryly on each rocky height,
Whose foothills' wooded convolutions rise
   Through a heavy, luminous air. And here
   Man might, as well as anywhere,
Combine his landscapes and philosophies.

There Sestri crammed into its littoral shelf
Seems motionless with distance ; motionless
Green flames pour up, the pines and cypresses
   Beyond the stream. The stream itself
Ripples and ripens to a falling sun
   Whose light makes metal at this hour
   Its golden froth of leaf and flower.
A dragonfly is basking on a stone.

Foam spurts between the pebbles ; currents swirl ;
It slides, a shining film, over rock
Smooth as itself, or into pools of dark.
   Where wood and sea and sky and hill
Give static broad simplicities, its course
   At once more complex and more simple
   Appears to thought as an example,
Like the complex, simple movement of great verse.

Gaze in that liquid crystal ; let it run,
Some simple, fluent structure of the all,
No many-corridored dark Escorial,
   But, poem or stream, a Parthenon :

The clear completeness of a gnomic rhyme ;
    Or, off the beat of pure despair
    But purer to the subtle ear,
The assonance of eternity with time.

How would it come ? This war gave nothing. If
No abstract thought can generate its laws
Unless some special impulse cracks or thaws
    The present icefields of belief :
— Perhaps from the strange new telepathic data,
    Or when the first craft, fairly soon,
    Its rockets flaring, eases down
To total strangeness under Deimos' glitter.

Till then, or till forever, those who've sought
Philosophies like verse, evoking verse,
Must take, as I beneath these junipers,
    Empiric rules of joy and thought,
And be content to break the idiot calm ;
    While many poems that dare not guide
    Yet bring the violent world inside
Some girl's ephemeral happiness and charm.

III

WAR AND AFTER

Offre une brebis noire à la noire tempête.
A. CHÉNIER

Posillipo: 1944

MINGLING the sea and the dawn
He stood inside his happy senses
In the green-and-white light and the summer
   air
Under two pines on the rocky shore
By the sea's blue lawn.

O Tritons and nymphs of the sea,
Come to him from the blue and fresh
Mind of that Sicilian poet and sing
Of a clear delight under the wave's wing
For the unhappy and free.

But let him return
To the hollows of the day
With the sensual lyric still in his veins,
To the arenas where in brilliant hearts and
   brains
The lives burn, burn.

Love and War

In the iron gardens the lilac high explosive . . .
There is always error rhyming in my veins,
The perfect colour of the echo stains
The images that try to stay impassive.

For the mouth must sing. It cannot sing about
Nothing, nor about the War, not only
That the brilliance of the echo makes it lonely
But that it needs more pleasure and more doubt.

So it sings, as usual, about a person
Round whom the echoes and the fighting swarm
Into a new and inconsistent version
Of things so often sung before.

— The heart tries never to deceive the poem,
But it changes, as her image changes, into War.

Poem in 1944

No, I cannot write the poem of war,
Neither the colossal dying nor the local scene,
A platoon asleep and dreaming of girls' warmth
Or by the petrol-cooker scraping out a laughter.
— Only the images that are not even nightmare :
A globe encrusted with a skin of seaweed,
Or razors at the roots.   The heart is no man's prism
To cast a frozen shadow down the streaming future ;
At most a cold slipstream of empty sorrow,
The grapes and melody of a dreamed love
Or a vague roar of courage.
                              No, I am not
The meeting point of event and vision, where the poem
Bursts into flame, and the heart's engine
Takes on the load of these broken years and lifts it.
I am not even the tongue and the hand that write
The dissolving sweetness of a personal view
Like those who now in greater luck and liberty
Are professionally pitiful or heroic. . . .

Into what eye to imagine the vista pouring
Its violent treasures ? For I must believe
That somewhere the poet is working who can handle
The flung world and his own heart.   To him I say
The little I can.   I offer him the debris
Of five years' undirected storm in self and Europe,
And my love.   Let him take it for what it's worth
In this poem scarcely made and already forgotten.

Caserta

WATER on bronze postures, a trickle of light
Suggests the slipping arm to the held sight ;
The statues in the fountains are almost moving,
Fauns ready to fall into the groove of loving.

It is a moment, a view from the top of a war.
He became a faun the moment he saw
The nymph immobile in the metal grove.
Her delicate shoulder carries a living dove.

O the slim bronze body can never be woken.
The dove flies. But its myth is not quite broken ;
Though behind it the war is as real as ever,
Is it to be a phoenix to the lover ?

Caught by quick fire in the sharp air's mesh
Can the grace remain in its raw roasting flesh
As in its flight beak, entrail and plume
Historic flames consume ?

A Minor Front

THE bridge attributed to Belisarius
Is blown, and we cross the stream on foot
Towards the little town.
                              Absolute power
Has receded like a tide from the Thracian hills
And the people reappears, a streaming rock
Surrounded by dead monsters.
                              Across the Struma
The German outposts can be seen, and their patrols
Still cross the river almost unopposed.
For the retreat was caused by pressure elsewhere
And here no force of partisans can yet
Resist them.   Half a dozen towns
Still lie in a no-man's-land which small patrols
Alone can enter.
                       The clouds appear
Fully created in the Aegean sky
And ahead of us the stony and half-empty
Struma glistens.
                       Among the buildings
(Not too badly wrecked) people are moving.
An old man, carrying a wooden bucket
Full of goat's milk, staggers to his neighbour's.
— The quick withdrawal of that violent empire
Has left a vacuum of rule.   Government is dead ;
And after the executions by patrols the tired survivors
Learn, for a few days, to work together, to live.
The best are in the mountains with the partisans
Or rotting in Salonika jail.   The worst come out
To loot or denounce.   And among the others only,
Mediocre and stupid, in small and selfish cities,

Half-suffocated by starvation and disease,
The free life of the holiday camp arises.
Very dimly through a host of more immediate noises
They faintly hear the music of the stateless future
Like a distant waterfall.
                              But there is too much.
Too much confusion ! Too much metal !
They have gazed too long into a mirror of Europe
And seen the Minotaur reflections gnash their teeth,
And they cannot keep their eyes on the green star
Nor listen to the bells.
                              The sky glitters, burning coldly.
The moment is losing its illumination ;
The world of politics and rifles reappears ;
In Seres, Drama, Sidhirokastron, life will revert
To the visionless present.
                              We lower our field-glasses,
And walk back to the far end of the village,
And pull out our rations and begin to eat,
As by the failing light we try to interpret
The gilt inscription on the public monument
In front of which, their hands still tied behind them,
The bodies of two gendarmes lie in the street.

Arion

DEATH and the sea transcended verbal shape.

He gazed at the olive-green unsmooth water, a salt pyre.
To die was more dreadful in his strong imagination,
But through its exalted centre he foresaw an escape.

Oh, the sailors realised the solemnity of the occasion :
Dressed in his ritual clothing, holding the lyre,
He sang an appropriate poem, and when it was done he
Came to the business of the day, was flung in the sea.

No one knows quite what his words were. Fragments of
      song
Picked up later from sailors in harbourside taverns
Do not sound authentic. And other singers, unfree
For lack of faith or intellectual strength or money,
Have since invented the dolphin for which they all long.

But perhaps as he unhooked his golden collar, ready,
A dolphin on its natural ways, or tempest-driven,
Really appeared and then vanished into the waves
Leaving for a moment an extra streak of foam
To be scattered at once by the splash of his plunging body.

And sailors, and after them poets, made the best of the
      story
And for ever distorted and fixed the inadequate data
But the truth is : even his corpse was not swept ashore.
      He,
After a brief agony, sank into calmer water
And with the manuscripts of his best and latest poems
Was rolled by the groundswell through its deepest caves.

On the Danube

(i)

THE convicts working on the frontier forts
Have been marched back.   The palpable cool air
Of evening lies round me now.   A single peasant
Passes unsteadily, reeking of plum brandy,
And then I am alone.

                The day pauses.   The great river
Slides softly by towards the delta and the sea ;
And now the sun strikes from an unaccustomed angle
And the light changes :

                    always at this hour
And in such scenery I wait for revelation,
Under a sky as pale as mother-of-pearl.
It is not that this pure moment can admit
A supernatural vision to the unclear heart,
But it hides the worn planet with its freshness ;
The light is no more absolute, but only
Closer to some untried colour of the air,
And there flickers round the horizons of my heart
The brilliance that precedes a greater brilliance.

(ii)

The winds of Europe and of tragedy
Are filling the sails of poetry here and everywhere.
And I wonder now in what tall uncaused singer
This rich and bitter land warms out.

                      Last night
In a little inn beside the landing-stage
A young man was writing verses at a table
And eating sturgeon stuffed with aubergines.

And perhaps he was the poet for whom the Balkans wait,
Though this is hardly likely.
                              The day before
I saw him reading Marx on a bench beside the river,
The witty laboured blue-prints for perfected anarchy,
Now legal in this country.   (The social sky
Holds only now his dialectic for its sun,
But I find a shade by the poetic tree
Under a moon of love.)
                        Night has fallen,
A young heron rises awkwardly into the air
Under the vague starlight, heading west.
The river ripples as some big fish dives.
And I walk back to the inn.
                              The moon is rising.

(iii)

I stumble over a machine-gun tripod
Half-buried in the sand.   It is now almost eight months
Since the S.S. Regiment 'Turkestan'
Was brought to battle here, surrounded and destroyed,
And a cold complexity of violence still
Lies heavy on this broken continent,
Which these bronze waters and this natural night
Can never answer.
                    Yet here I am alone and far
From the brilliance of the fighting ideologies,
And I think of a girl in a small provincial town
Looking through a spring rain and imagining love.

Lament for a Landing Craft

FOUR fathoms under the green
Water, canted between
Two rocks, half on its side
Under the lowest low tide

The flat hull now dimly seen
Bore an armoured machine
Towards the golden wide
Beach, but the forts replied,

Till the swell and the fury were clean
Gone, and it entered a scene
Of soundless shimmer and glide
Heavy with myth. Time died.

And the years' and the waters' sheen
Smoothed out this image, serene
Enough, perhaps, to provide
For eternity's moods, and to guide.

Men escaped, or have been
Made smooth bone by the keen
Teeth. And the weeds hide
Skull, keel, plan, pride.

IV

THE BALKANS

Sunset under Vitosha

FOR T.

THE song tries often to give the true relation
Between the human figure and the face of nature,
To find in the one the other's hidden features.
— It sometimes seems to find an explanation.

But now in the sea-green air and the soft light
It leaves aside your beauty and your kindness,
Its strangeness strikes down through habitual blindness,
Its unknown colours waken and excite.

A sudden absolute silence from the birds,
The sycamore become an orange fire
And every shadow turned to depths of blue :

How can this strangeness shape the whole desire
Into that other beauty which is you ?

What does it mean ?   Where are its words ?

Near Sliven

THE whole range rises like a monument
Out of the Tundja valley.   The cool air strokes
    my cheek
Stirred by the breeze's hand
Like lightly perfumed water.
A trace of distant nimbus hangs on that
    eastern peak.

It is so high here that the sultry weather
Becomes as rare and delicate as spring.
And the plum-trees tremble
In a mirror's clearness
Where the shining stream echoes the evening.

I imagine this valley, with its rose-fields,
In a pure calm always : in December's snow
A quiet snow glade
In the windy mountains' arms.
But I have not been here in winter, and I do
    not know.

Lamartine at Philippopolis

DAWN, pale and hot, came through the Turkish blind.
He opened it and stood and looked at Thrace,
The plain and town conveying to his mind
Such truth as he could draw from fact and place.

Caught like clear water by a curving range
— The blurred rose of Rhodope to the south —
Its very clarity grown strong and strange
The early air came sweetly to his mouth.

Clear light diffused by the outcropping rock
Above the straight Maritza's ochre flow
Entered his heart. And did it there unlock
The politics of fifteen years, and show

82754

The blue and breaking wave on which he soared ;
His songs' clear motives wreck the ancient curse ;
When history gathered to a single chord
And all the rostra spoke heroic verse ?

Or could he in the inn's reviving stink,
The haggling envies rising from the street,
Suspect his gold conceptions' broken link,
The tyrant's pension and the poem's defeat ?

Pliska

HISTORY again, but different : the ancient capital
From which Bulgaria draws its age and fullness ;
    The early Khans from here
    Struck their forgotten empire
    Across the Balkan map,
And Krum drank from Nicephorus' gilded skull.

And though a barren nationalism may rant and raise
These giant stones as engines of aggressive war,
    These tombs and temples give
    A real pride and life
    And a felt depth
Beyond the lost five hundred years of Beys.

Their weight can hold that wildness to a fair control
At single points like this, or where, ten miles away,
    History roars from the rocks at Madara
    Where Krum puts a spear through the lion's
        shoulder
    In a fanfare of inscriptions,
And an ancient honest people becomes a living
        whole.

Aegean

SEA and evening : in the sky
Colours of honey, ice and lime.
    I lie in the coastal grove
Of ilexes and cork-trees on the dry
And aromatic ground, relaxed into
My brain and body, not concerned with love.

Though with you I have often seen
Occasional objects, branches and stones,
    Glowing with love in your eyes,
Now a more physically haunting dream
Grasps me in this seascape as the summer
Lightning drones around these evening skies.

Till I am saturated with
The impersonal magic which long ago
    From women loosed dryads to roam
Through groves like these.
                 — In such a sexual myth
You were the first and only one to show me
The relation between a woman and a poem.

Messemvria at Noon

HERE is the little building-crowded island
Joined by a narrow causeway to the land ;
Rich brick-reds, and pale browns and whites.

For more than two millennia in this narrow space,
Since the Megarans laid the first foundations,
Houses and churches have been always rising
And falling, like seasonal plants.
                                    In the little square
Labourers are digging out the cellars
For some new building. They cut through human strata,
Layers of carved stone and brick, of arch and pillar,
And ghost-talk breaks out from inscriptions
Gagged for centuries. History speaks
With a stone tongue, and also in the gestures
Of fishermen in the little inn repeating
Their ancestors' attitudes and even words.

Back on the mainland now we turn
Where the wind hisses through the sawgrass,
Among scattered light-blue flowers, high up
Among the pale green vegetation of the dunes
And the pale sand, and under a pale blue sky ;
An empty grassland stretches towards the hills,
And far into the distance goes
The long white curve of empty beach
                                    And the town
Shines, a concentrate of human living
Set in a desert of natural beauty here.

The heat-haze crystallizes to a prism
Through which we see it clearly, caught in a pale gold

Except for a darkness by the northern cliff
Where the curve of a Byzantine church cupola
Gives from the shadow a single striking light
                              And turning left we see
Far down the bay and visible for miles
The blinding white of a gull.

By Rail through Istria

LIMESTONE and pine : a dry country.
The train curves downhill through the early light
    Towards another day and sea
    That put before the sensitized light
Complexity that hints of symmetry,
Fit background for the hard thoughts' resolution.
A trace of haze softens the sky's blueness
And this clarity and freshness once again
Present the problem in its old quick newness :
The usual attempt to make perfection plain,
To reduce the world to reason and to poetry ;
    To let the landscape's magic impulse
    Flow like a stream to bear the symbols
Through a poem as strictly driven as this train.

    But the poems are waterlogged and lift
Too slowly to the swell of the idea.
    Today I can only begin to clear
    The ground, to note the general drift
Of a poem's necessity. It is not enough
To find a mood to ride the thrust of love,
Nor should the detail of this rock and tree
Fade in a single brilliant light, be lost
In imprecisions of immensity,
Nor golden images proliferate
Except as phosphorescence forming on
    A sea of close secretive strength.
    And by such strictness perhaps at length
I could merge joy with precision ; and create.

    And now we run by the sea,
A streak of blue and shimmer on the shore

Above which whitish sea-birds soar
 — Specks to an unresolving eye.
And what, for example, is the strict relation
Between the sea which in the last verse figured
As abstract image in a thought's defence,
And this emotive single clear impression
On the visual nerve ; or with the real liquid
Full of weeds and plankton where the fish
Are dumb and the myth-illustrating dolphins
 Grunt, they say, like pigs ? Does some
 Answer pend, or would the poem
Just turn to logic or to gibberish ?

 And now in Monfalcone station
A dark girl, motionless, distracts the heart
From that : its light remembers concentration,
Till single objects fluoresce exact
Radiance to illuminate and illustrate
 The philosophic whole. To sing
 Might flower out of anything :
I learn to seek the fruitful thing or act.

In the Rhodope

THE poem tries to speak of the heart
And to relate it to the natural plectrum
Which plucks so clear a note out of its sunlight,
To make its vague, neglected virtues flare
From the ocean and air.

But how does the poem come?
Its voices bubbling from a pool of darkness
To a deliberate fruit of grapes and peaches?
Or striking a horror and a melody at night
Down corridors of dead light?

And how does it distort?
Like the pearl-diver's hand trembling under water
Towards his stone of food and beauty? Or
Absolute mirage into a lonely eye
Out of the swan sky?

— Let me write one more poem,
About this lake at night, black with a golden ice,
Or some green transparent atmosphere at daybreak
Made beautiful by that strange illumination
That poets are always working to bring out
— The colour of doubt.

PRINTED BY R. & R. CLARK, LTD., EDINBURGH